Dedication

This book is dedicated to God, who has given humanity the gift of knowledge and understanding, which has allowed us to accomplish amazing things.

This book is also dedicated to all company CEOs and business ow ners in all industries.

Your forward

thinking ideas, tireless efforts, and unwavering resolve are advanci ng society and influencing our future.

We are grateful that you have motivated us all to aim high.

Preface

Artificial Intelligence is revolutionizing the way we live and work. It is rapidly changing industries, enabling greater efficiency, productivity, and profitability. As machines become increasingly sophisticated, it is only natural that they will play an ever more significant role in decision-making, including in the realm of business leadership.

The Rise of the AI CEOs explores this fascinating topic, charting the rise of intelligent machines in the boardroom and examining the potential implications for businesses and society as a whole. Through a series of interviews and case studies, we delve into the experiences of those at the forefront of this trend, seeking to understand their perspectives on the opportunities and challenges presented by AI in the C-suite.

As the world changes at a breakneck pace, it is essential to stay abreast of the latest trends and technologies. This book aims to provide a comprehensive overview of the role that AI is currently playing and is likely to play in the future of business leadership. It is written for entrepreneurs, executives, and anyone with an interest in the future of work and the impact of technology on society.

The authors hope that The Rise of the AI CEOs will contribute to the ongoing discussion around AI and its place in the business world. We invite you to join us on this journey of discovery, and we look forward to hearing your thoughts and insights on this critical issue.

THE RISE OF THE AI CEOs

Freeson Eze

Contents

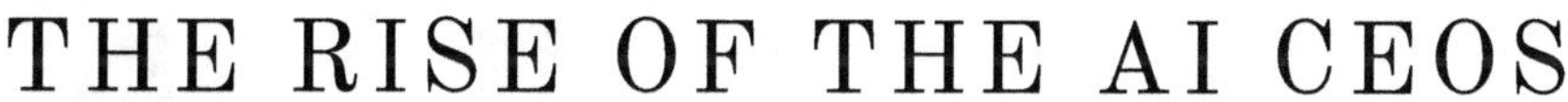

THE RISE OF THE AI CEOS

ACKNOWLEDGMENTS

With great appreciation, I would like to thank everyone who helped make *The Rise of the AI CEOs: How Machine Learning is Changing the C-Suite* possible. First and foremost, I want to express my gratitude to my family for all of their support and encouragement along this journey. Your comprehension and tolerance have been really helpful.

My sincere gratitude goes out to the authorities and industry leaders in artificial intelligence and business who so kindly shared their knowledge and experiences. The content of this book has been greatly influenced by your Sknowledge.

My editor and the publishing team deserve a special thank you for their invaluable help and experience in making this project a reality. We really appreciate all of your effort and commitment.

I also want to express my gratitude to my friends and coworkers for their encouragement, motivation, and advice.. This work has been enhanced by your discussions and points of view.

In closing, I'd want to pay tribute to all of the pioneers and inventors in the field of artificial intelligence. Your innovative work never stops challenging and inspiring us all. This book is an homage to your work and to the way business technology will develop in the future.

I am grateful that you are all a part of this adventure.

.

Introduction

The Rise of the Artificial Intelligence (AI) Chief Executive Officer (CEO): How Machine Learning is Changing the C-Suite"

What is the C-Suite?
The C-Suite refers to the highest level of senior executives in a company, typically consisting of the CEO, CFO (Chief Financial Officer), COO (Chief Operating Officer), CMO (Chief Marketing Officer), and other high-ranking executives. These individuals are responsible for making strategic decisions that shape the direction and vision of the company, and they are typically involved in setting goals, managing budgets, and overseeing the day-to-day operations of the organization. The term "C-Suite" is derived from the first letter of each executive's title, which typically begins with the letter "C."

AI is revolutionizing the business landscape, and its impact is being felt across all levels of organizations. From automating repetitive tasks to predicting customer behavior, AI is changing the way businesses operate and compete in the market. The CEO, as the top leader in a company, is not immune to the effects of AI. In fact, AI is fundamentally changing the role of the CEO, requiring new skills and perspectives to be an effective leader in an AI-driven business environment.

"The Rise of the AI CEO: How Machine Learning is Changing the C-Suite" is a book that explores the impact of AI on the role of the CEO and how leaders can navigate this rapidly changing landscape. In this book, we delve into the key skills and attributes that successful AI CEOs possess, such as the ability to interpret and leverage data, adapt to rapidly changing technological landscapes, and cultivate a culture of innovation and experimentation.

The book also addresses the challenges and risks associated with the use of AI in business leadership, such as the potential for bias in AI decision-making and the ethical considerations that arise with the use of AI in hiring and workforce management. Through case studies, interviews with AI CEOs, and expert analysis, "The Rise of the AI CEO" provides valuable insights for current and aspiring business leaders on how to navigate the AI-driven future of the C-Suite.

The world of business is rapidly changing, and leaders who fail to adapt to new technologies and trends risk being left behind. As AI becomes increasingly integrated into business operations, it is essential for CEOs to understand its potential and limitations and to develop the skills and mindset necessary to lead their organizations effectively in an AI-driven future.

"The Rise of the AI CEO" is an essential read for anyone interested in understanding the intersection of business and AI and how the two are transforming the future of work and leadership. Through this book, we hope to provide practical guidance and inspiration for CEOs and other business leaders looking to stay ahead of the curve in this new era of technological disruption.

As we embark on this journey to explore the future of business leadership in the age of AI, it is important to acknowledge that the impact of AI is not limited to just one aspect of the business world. AI is transforming the way we think about customer engagement, marketing, supply chain management, and even our approach to product development. As a result, the CEO's role is becoming increasingly complex, and the ability to leverage AI technology has become a crucial component of effective leadership.

In "The Rise of the AI CEO," we examine the unique challenges and opportunities that AI presents to CEOs and how leaders can harness the power of AI to drive growth, improve efficiency, and foster innovation. We explore the various ways in which AI is being integrated into business operations, including machine learning algorithms that can predict customer behavior, automated decision-making systems that can streamline operations, and chat-bots that can provide 24/7 customer support.

The book also addresses the ethical considerations surrounding AI and the potential for bias in decision-making. As AI systems become more sophisticated, it is crucial for CEOs to ensure that their organizations are using AI in a responsible and ethical manner and that they are aware of the potential risks and limitations of the technology.

Ultimately, "The Rise of the AI CEO" is a call to action for business leaders to embrace the transformative power of AI and to develop the skills and mindset necessary to lead their organizations in a rapidly changing technological landscape. With practical insights and real-world examples, this book is a valuable resource for CEOs and other business leaders looking to stay ahead of the curve and succeed in the age of AI.

1

Chapter:1

The impact of technology on the future of work

We will explores how technological advancements such as automation, artificial intelligence, and the Internet of Things are transforming the world of work.

The impact of technology on the future of work is a topic that has generated a lot of interest and concern in recent years. As technological advancements continue to accelerate, many people are wondering what the future of work will look like and how it will be affected by these changes.

One of the most significant ways in which technology is transforming the world of work is through automation. Advances in robotics and other automated technologies have made it possible to automate many tasks that were previously performed by human workers. This has led to increased efficiency and productivity, but it has also raised concerns about job displacement and the impact on workers who may be replaced by machines.

Another technology that is having a significant impact on the future of work is artificial intelligence (AI). AI is being used to automate a wide range of tasks, from data entry to customer service to financial analysis. This has the potential to improve efficiency and reduce costs for businesses, but it also raises questions about the impact on workers who may be replaced by AI-powered systems.

The Internet of Things (IoT) is another technology that is transforming the world of work. The IoT refers to the growing network of interconnected devices and sensors that can communicate with one another. This technology is being used to improve efficiency and productivity in a wide range of industries, from manufacturing to healthcare to logistics.

While these technological advancements are undoubtedly transforming the world of work, there are also concerns about the impact on workers and society as a whole. For example, there are concerns about job displacement and the potential for increased inequality as some workers are replaced by machines. There are also concerns about the impact on mental health and well-being as workers are expected to be constantly connected and available through their mobile devices and other technologies.

Overall, the impact of technology on the future of work is a complex and multifaceted issue. While there are certainly benefits to be gained from technological advancements, it is important to consider the potential risks and challenges as well. As we continue to navigate this rapidly changing landscape, it will be important to work toward solutions that ensure that the benefits of technology are shared fairly and equitably among all members of society.

In addition to the concerns about job displacement and inequality, the impact of technology on the future of work is also likely to have a significant impact on the nature of work itself. For example, automation and AI are likely to lead to a shift toward more specialized and highly skilled jobs as routine and repetitive tasks are automated. This means that workers will need to develop new skills and be prepared to adapt to changing job requirements.

Another potential impact of technology on the future of work is the increasing importance of remote work and flexible work arrangements. The COVID-19 pandemic has accelerated the trend toward remote work, and many companies are now embracing this model as a way to reduce costs and increase productivity. However, this shift also raises questions about the future of traditional office-based work and the potential impact on communities that rely on these jobs.

The impact of technology on the future of work is also likely to have a significant impact on education and training. As the nature of work changes, workers will need to develop new skills and knowledge to remain competitive in the job market. This means that education and training programs will need to adapt to these changing needs, and workers will need to be able to access these programs throughout their careers.

Finally, the impact of technology on the future of work is likely to have a significant impact on the overall economy. As automation and AI continue to advance, there is the potential for significant gains in productivity and efficiency. However, these gains may not be evenly distributed, and there is a risk that they could lead to increased inequality if they are not accompanied by policies and programs that ensure that everyone benefits.

The impact of technology on the future of work is a complicated and multifaceted issue that will have far-reaching consequences for workers, businesses, and society as a whole. While these technological advancements pose some risks and challenges, they also present opportunities for innovation and growth. As we navigate this rapidly changing landscape, it will be critical to work toward solutions that ensure that the benefits of technology are distributed fairly and equitably among all members of society.

Automation and the Future of Work.

Automation is one of the most significant technological advancements that is transforming the future of work. The use of robots and other automated systems has enabled businesses to achieve higher levels of efficiency and productivity, leading to increased profits and economic growth. However, it has also raised concerns about the impact on jobs and the potential displacement of human workers.

Advancements in automation have already had a profound impact on industries such as manufacturing and logistics. Automation has enabled factories and warehouses to achieve levels of efficiency and productivity that were previously impossible, leading to lower costs and higher profits. However, this has also led to a reduction in the number of jobs available for human workers.

As automation technology continues to advance, it is likely to have an impact on a wider range of industries. For example, the use of autonomous vehicles and drones is likely to transform the transportation and delivery industries, while the use of robotic systems in healthcare could revolutionize the way that medical procedures are performed.

While automation has the potential to improve efficiency and productivity, it also raises concerns about the impact on jobs and the workforce. As machines become more capable of performing tasks that were previously done by humans, there is the potential for significant job displacement. This could lead to increased inequality and social unrest as workers who are replaced by machines struggle to find new employment opportunities.

Another potential impact of automation on the future of work is the shift toward more specialized and highly skilled jobs. As routine and repetitive tasks are increasingly automated, there is likely to be a greater demand for workers who can perform complex and creative tasks that are difficult for machines to replicate. This means that workers will need to develop new skills and be prepared to adapt to changing job requirements.

Furthermore, the rise of automation is likely to lead to a greater emphasis on human-machine collaboration. As machines become more capable of performing tasks previously performed by humans, workers who can collaborate with these machines and ensure that they are used effectively will be in demand.

It will be crucial for education and training programs to adapt to the shifting demands of the workforce to address these changes. This could entail creating new curricula that emphasize the abilities that are most in demand in the age of automation, such as collaboration, critical thinking, and problem-solving. It might also entail the creation of fresh training curricula that aid employees in adjusting to shifting job demands and picking up new skills over the course of their careers.

Another potential solution to the challenges posed by automation is the development of new industries and job opportunities. As machines become more capable of performing routine and repetitive tasks, there will be a greater emphasis on the development of new industries and jobs that require human creativity and innovation. This could include industries such as the arts, entertainment, and design, as well as fields such as scientific research and engineering.

To address these concerns, it is important for policymakers and business leaders to work toward solutions that ensure that the benefits of automation are shared fairly and equitably. This may involve policies that support retraining and reskilling for workers who are displaced by automation as well as programs that promote the development of new industries and job opportunities.

In conclusion, automation is a technology that is transforming the future of work in profound ways. While there are certainly benefits to be gained from increased efficiency and productivity, it is important to consider the potential risks and challenges associated with job displacement and inequality. As we continue to navigate this rapidly changing landscape, it will be important to work toward solutions that ensure that the benefits of automation are shared fairly and equitably among all members of society.

The Rise of AI in the Workplace

AI is rapidly transforming the way that work is done across a wide range of industries. From healthcare to finance to manufacturing, AI is being used to automate tasks, analyze data, and improve decision-making processes. While there are certainly benefits to be gained from the use of AI in the workplace, there are also significant challenges and risks that must be addressed.

One of the primary benefits of AI in the workplace is its potential to improve efficiency and productivity. AI systems can be used to automate routine tasks, freeing up human workers to focus on more complex and creative tasks that are better suited to their skills and abilities. AI can also be used to analyze large amounts of data quickly and accurately, providing insights that can inform decision-making and drive business growth.

However, the use of AI in the workplace also raises concerns about job displacement and its impact on the workforce. As machines become more capable of performing tasks that were previously done by humans, there is the potential for significant job loss and displacement. This could lead to increased inequality and social unrest, particularly if workers who are displaced by AI are unable to find new employment opportunities.

Policymakers and business leaders must strive for solutions that guarantee the equitable distribution of AI benefits among all members of society. One possible solution is to implement policies that facilitate the retraining and re-skilling of workers who have lost their jobs due to AI, as well as programs that encourage the emergence of new industries and job opportunities.

Another potential challenge associated with the use of AI in the workplace is the ethical implications. AI systems are only as unbiased and impartial as the data they are trained on. This means that there is a risk of AI systems perpetuating and even amplifying existing biases and inequalities. For example, if an AI system is trained on data that is biased against certain groups of people, it may be more likely to make decisions that negatively impact those groups.

To address these ethical concerns, it will be important for businesses and policymakers to develop guidelines and regulations for the use of AI in the workplace. This may involve the development of ethical standards for the use of AI as well as regulations that ensure that AI systems are transparent and accountable.

In summary, the emergence of AI in the workplace is changing how work is done in a variety of industries. While there are unquestionably advantages to using AI, there are also sizable risks and challenges that must be taken into consideration. It will be crucial for policymakers and business leaders to work toward solutions that guarantee that the benefits of AI are shared fairly and equitably among all members of society and that AI is used ethically and responsibly as we continue to navigate this quickly changing landscape.

Skills Development and Training for the Future of Work

As the world of work continues to evolve rapidly, it is becoming increasingly important for individuals to develop new skills and competencies to remain competitive in the job market. The rise of automation, AI, and other technologies is transforming the nature of work, and many jobs that were once considered secure are now at risk of being automated or outsourced. To thrive in this new environment, workers must be able to adapt and develop new skills that are in demand.

One of the key skills that are becoming increasingly important in the modern workplace is digital literacy. As more and more tasks are being performed digitally, workers who can use digital tools effectively are at a significant advantage. This includes not only technical skills such as programming and data analysis but also the ability to use digital tools for communication, collaboration, and problem-solving.

Another important skill for the future of work is creativity. As machines become more capable of performing routine tasks, there is an increasing need for workers who can think outside the box and come up with innovative solutions to complex problems. This includes skills such as ideation, brainstorming, and design thinking.

In addition to these technical and creative skills, there is also a growing need for workers who possess emotional intelligence and other soft skills. These include skills such as communication, teamwork, leadership, and empathy. In a world where many jobs can be performed remotely, the ability to work effectively with others and to communicate clearly and persuasively is becoming increasingly important.

To help workers develop these skills, there are a variety of training and educational programs available. These range from traditional academic programs such as degrees and certifications to on-the-job training and apprenticeships to online courses and tutorials. Many employers are also investing in training programs for their employees to ensure that they have the skills they need to remain competitive in the marketplace.

One of the challenges in skill development and training for the future of work is ensuring that these programs are accessible to everyone. This includes individuals who may not have the financial resources to pursue traditional academic programs, as well as those who may not have access to high-quality training programs in their local area. To address these challenges, there are a variety of initiatives and programs that aim to make training and education more accessible and affordable for all.

Another challenge is ensuring that these programs are effective at developing the skills that are most in demand in the modern workplace. This requires collaboration between educators, employers, and policymakers to ensure that training programs are aligned with the needs of the job market and that they provide students with the skills and competencies they need to succeed.

As the nature of work continues to change, skill development and training are becoming more and more important in the modern workplace. To survive and succeed in this new environment, employees must be able to adapt and learn new skills. There are numerous education and training programs that can help with this, but it is crucial to make sure they are easily accessible, efficient, and in line with the demands of the labor market. By doing this, we can contribute to ensuring that workers have the tools necessary to succeed in the workplace of the future.

The Economic Implications of Technological Advancements on the Future of Work

Technological advancements such as automation, AI, and the IoT are rapidly transforming the world of work. While these advancements offer many benefits, they also raise significant economic concerns that need to be addressed to ensure a fair and prosperous future for all.

One of the most significant economic implications of technological advancements is the potential for job displacement. As machines become increasingly capable of performing tasks that were once the domain of human workers, many jobs are at risk of being automated or outsourced. This could lead to widespread unemployment and economic disruption, particularly in industries that are highly susceptible to automation, such as manufacturing, transportation, and retail.

However, it is important to note that technological advancements can also create new job opportunities and industries. For example, the rise of e-commerce has led to the emergence of new jobs in fields such as logistics, digital marketing, and software development. The key to ensuring a positive economic outcome is to ensure that workers have the skills and training they need to adapt to these new opportunities.

Another economic concern related to technological advancements is the potential for income inequality. As machines become increasingly capable of performing high-skilled tasks, there is a risk that the benefits of these advancements will accrue primarily to the owners of capital rather than to workers. This could lead to an even wider gap between the rich and poor, exacerbating existing economic disparities.

To address this concern, policymakers and business leaders must work together to ensure that the benefits of technological advancements are shared fairly and equitably. This may involve implementing policies such as progressive taxation, universal basic income, and worker protections that ensure that workers are not left behind in the transition to a more technologically advanced economy.

Another potential economic implication of technological advancements is the impact on wages and working conditions. As machines become increasingly capable of performing tasks that were once the domain of human workers, there is a risk that wages and working conditions will deteriorate. This could lead to widespread economic insecurity and a decline in living standards.

To address this concern, policymakers and business leaders must work together to ensure that workers are protected and empowered in the new economy. This may involve implementing policies such as minimum wage laws, collective bargaining rights, and worker protections that ensure that workers can earn a living wage and work in safe and healthy conditions.

Finally, there is a concern that technological advancements could lead to a decline in economic growth and productivity. While technological advancements have the potential to boost productivity and economic growth, there is also a risk that they could lead to a decline in these metrics if not managed properly. For example, if machines are used to perform tasks that are of low value, this could lead to a decline in productivity and economic growth.

This may involve implementing policies that promote the development of new industries and job opportunities, investing in research and development to ensure that technological advancements are used in a way that maximizes their potential benefits, and fostering a culture of innovation and entrepreneurship that encourages the development of new technologies and businesses.

In conclusion, technological advancements have significant economic implications for the future of work. While these advancements offer many benefits, they also raise significant economic concerns that need to be addressed to ensure a fair and prosperous future for all. By working together to address these concerns, policymakers and business leaders can help ensure that the benefits of technological advancements are shared fairly and equitably, that workers are protected and empowered in the new economy, and that technological advancements are used in a way that maximizes their potential benefits while minimizing their potential drawbacks.

2

Chapter: 2

The Evolving Role of the CEO in an artificial intelligence (AI)-driven Business Environment

Introduction

As the business landscape continues to evolve, the role of the CEO is changing in profound ways. Nowhere is this more evident than in the age of AI, where emerging technologies are transforming the way we work, communicate, and make decisions. In this chapter, we will explore the evolving role of the CEO in an AI-driven business environment.

We will begin by examining the new challenges and opportunities that AI presents for CEOs. From unlocking new sources of data to automating routine tasks, AI has the potential to revolutionize the way businesses operate. However, it also presents a range of challenges, from the need to develop new skill sets to the potential for bias and other ethical concerns.

We will then turn our attention to the key competencies that CEOs need to develop to succeed in this new landscape. From data literacy to strategic thinking, the skills required of a successful CEO are evolving rapidly. We will explore how CEOs can develop these competencies, from training and education to working closely with AI experts and other members of their teams.

Ultimately, this chapter will offer a comprehensive overview of the evolving role of the CEO in an AI-driven business environment. Whether you are a CEO looking to stay ahead of the curve or a business professional seeking to understand the latest trends in AI and leadership, this chapter will provide valuable insights and practical advice.

The chapter will also delve into how AI is changing the decision-making process and the implications for the CEO's role in setting strategy, evaluating risks and opportunities, and leading the organization. We will explore the potential of AI to help CEOs make faster and more informed decisions, as well as the risks of relying too heavily on automated decision-making systems.

Additionally, we will examine the importance of leadership in an AI-driven world. The chapter will explore the key competencies that CEOs need to develop to lead effectively in an AI-driven environment, from fostering a culture of innovation to building diverse and interdisciplinary teams. We will also examine case studies of successful AI implementation in organizations, highlighting the critical role that leadership played in driving these initiatives forward.

Finally, the chapter will examine the ethical considerations of AI implementation and the importance of responsible AI leadership. We will explore the potential for bias and other ethical concerns and discuss how CEOs can promote ethical AI practices throughout their organizations.

Overall, this chapter aims to provide a comprehensive overview of the evolving role of the CEO in an AI-driven business environment. By exploring the challenges and opportunities of AI implementation and providing practical advice on developing the key competencies needed to succeed, this chapter will be an essential resource for CEOs and business professionals looking to stay ahead of the curve in the age of AI.

The Changing Nature of Decision-Making

In today's business landscape, the role of AI in decision-making is rapidly evolving. As organizations increasingly rely on data-driven insights to guide their strategy, the CEO's role in decision-making is transforming.

The rise of AI is rapidly changing the decision-making process in organizations, and this has significant implications for the CEO's role in setting strategy, evaluating risks and opportunities, and leading the organization.

One way that AI is changing the decision-making process is through its ability to analyze vast amounts of data quickly and accurately. With AI, organizations can access valuable insights that would otherwise be difficult or impossible to obtain, leading to more informed decision-making. However, it is essential to recognize that AI has limitations, and decisions should not be based solely on data-driven insights. The CEO must ensure that AI-driven insights are balanced with other factors, such as market trends, customer needs, and organizational capabilities.

The use of AI is also changing the CEO's role in setting strategy. By leveraging AI, organizations can develop more sophisticated and accurate forecasting models, leading to better strategic decisions. However, it is crucial to recognize that the CEO's judgment is still essential in evaluating strategic options. AI can provide a snapshot of the market at a given moment, but it cannot replace the CEO's intuition and experience in evaluating strategic options.

AI is also changing the way organizations evaluate risks and opportunities. AI can help identify risks and opportunities that might otherwise go unnoticed, providing valuable insights into potential risks and opportunities. However, the CEO's role in evaluating these risks and opportunities is still critical. The CEO must balance AI-driven insights with their intuition and experience in evaluating risks and opportunities to make informed decisions.

Lastly, the rise of AI is changing the nature of leadership in organizations. The CEO is evolving from being a decision-maker to a facilitator, enabling teams to make data-driven decisions. The CEO's role is to foster a culture of experimentation and learning in the organization, which is essential for successful AI implementation. Effective communication and transparency in decision-making are also crucial in situations where AI is driving insights.

In addition to the implications discussed above, AI is also changing the role of the CEO in terms of talent management. With the increasing use of AI, there is a growing demand for professionals with AI skills and expertise. The CEO needs to identify the skills that are required for the organization's AI strategy and make the necessary investments in talent development.

Furthermore, the rise of AI has the potential to change the structure of the organization. As AI increasingly automates routine tasks, organizations are likely to become flatter with fewer layers of management. This means that the CEO's role in leading and managing the organization may shift, with a greater focus on managing cross-functional teams and facilitating collaboration across the organization.

Another key consideration for the CEO is the ethical implications of AI-driven decision-making. AI algorithms are only as unbiased as the data they are trained on, and there is a risk of perpetuating existing biases in decision-making. The CEO needs to ensure that AI is used ethically and responsibly and that it aligns with the organization's values.

The CEO's role in managing change is crucial in the context of AI-driven decision-making. The adoption of AI will inevitably require changes in processes, organizational structures, and culture. The CEO must manage these changes effectively to ensure that the organization can leverage AI successfully.

As a result of the rise of AI, decision-making has changed significantly, which has important ramifications for the CEO's role in formulating strategy, assessing risks and opportunities, leading the organization, managing talent, and ensuring AI is used ethically and responsibly. To effectively lead the organization in an AI-driven business environment, the CEO must adjust to these changes and acquire the necessary skills.

As businesses increasingly turn to AI for decision-making, it is important to remember that AI-driven insights are just one piece of the puzzle. While AI can provide valuable data-driven insights, it is important to balance these insights with other factors that are critical to the success of the business. Market trends, customer needs, and organizational capabilities are just a few examples of factors that should be taken into account when making decisions.

For example, while AI may be able to identify patterns in customer behavior, it is important to also consider the context behind those patterns. Understanding the underlying motivations and needs of customers can help businesses tailor their offerings to better meet their needs and differentiate themselves from competitors.

Similarly, while AI can provide valuable insights into market trends and opportunities, it is important to also consider the organization's capabilities and resources. Pursuing opportunities that are not aligned with the organization's strengths can lead to costly mistakes and missed opportunities.

Ultimately, the CEO's role is to ensure that the organization can leverage AI effectively while also considering these other important factors. This requires a balance between data-driven decision-making and strategic thinking, which is a key competency for CEOs in an AI-driven business environment. By balancing AI-driven insights with other factors, CEOs can make more informed decisions that drive the long-term success of their organization.

AI is rapidly transforming the way businesses operate, and one area where it is having a significant impact is in the CEO's role in setting strategy. With the help of AI, organizations are now able to develop more sophisticated and accurate forecasting models, which can provide insights into market trends and consumer behavior.

These insights can be incredibly valuable in informing strategic decisions, as they enable CEOs to make data-driven decisions and identify opportunities that might otherwise have been missed. For example, an AI-powered analysis of market trends might reveal an emerging market that is ripe for expansion or identify shifts in consumer behavior that can inform product development and marketing strategies.

However, it is important to note that AI should be seen as a tool to augment the CEO's judgment, not replace it. While AI can provide valuable insights, it can only provide a snapshot of the market at a given moment and cannot take into account the complexities of the business environment or the unique strengths and weaknesses of the organization.

The CEO's role in evaluating strategic options is still crucial, as they are responsible for making the final decisions based on a range of factors, including the organization's capabilities, resources, and long-term goals. Moreover, they must also consider the potential risks and challenges associated with any strategic decision and be prepared to adjust course if necessary.

The Importance of Data Literacy for CEOs

In today's AI-driven business landscape, data is the new gold. With the advent of big data and machine learning, organizations can now collect, analyze, and derive insights from vast amounts of information. As a result, CEOs need to be fluent in data analysis and interpretation to make informed decisions that drive business success. In this chapter, we will explore the importance of data literacy for CEOs and how they can develop this essential competency.

The importance of data literacy for CEOs cannot be overstated in today's AI-driven business landscape.

In today's rapidly evolving business landscape, data is increasingly becoming the lifeblood of organizations. With the growth of big data and machine learning, organizations can now collect and analyze vast amounts of information to derive valuable insights that can help drive business success. However, this flood of data can be overwhelming and difficult to manage without the proper knowledge and tools. This is where data literacy comes in.

Data literacy is the ability to read, understand, create, and communicate data as information. It is a fundamental skill that enables individuals to navigate the increasingly data-driven business world. For CEOs, in particular, data literacy is crucial to making informed decisions that drive business success in the age of AI.

One of the most significant benefits of data literacy for CEOs is the ability to use data-driven insights to guide strategic planning. Data can provide insights into market trends, customer behavior, and competitor activity, allowing CEOs to make informed decisions about where to invest resources and which opportunities to pursue. By incorporating data into the strategic planning process, CEOs can make more informed decisions that are more likely to yield positive outcomes.

In addition to guiding strategic planning, data literacy can also help CEOs identify new opportunities. Data can uncover hidden trends and patterns that may not be immediately apparent and help CEOs identify new markets, products, or services that they may not have considered before. By being data literate, CEOs can stay ahead of the curve and be more proactive in identifying new opportunities that can help drive business growth.

Another way data literacy can benefit CEOs is by enabling them to innovate more effectively. With access to data, CEOs can better understand customer needs and preferences and use that information to create new products and services that meet those needs. This can lead to greater innovation and differentiation, allowing the organization to stand out in a crowded marketplace.

However, despite the many benefits of data literacy, it is important to note that it is not just about being able to analyze data. It is also about being able to communicate the insights derived from that data effectively. CEOs need to be able to explain the implications of data to stakeholders within the organization and make data-driven decisions that are easily understood by everyone. This requires not only technical expertise but also effective communication skills.

In conclusion, data literacy is essential for CEOs to make informed decisions that drive business success in the age of AI. It empowers them to use data-driven insights to guide strategic planning, identify new opportunities, and innovate more effectively. By developing this essential competency, CEOs can stay ahead of the curve and make better decisions that benefit their organizations and stakeholders.

The need for strategic thinking

With the rise of AI, CEOs must be strategic in how they leverage this technology to drive business success. This means developing a clear vision for how AI fits into their organization's overall strategy and understanding its potential impact on their industry.

Strategic thinking in the age of AI involves considering how AI can be used to create new products and services, streamline operations, and enhance customer experiences. CEOs must also consider the potential risks and challenges associated with AI, such as cyber security threats, ethical considerations, and the impact on the workforce.

In addition to understanding the potential applications of AI in their organization, CEOs must also be aware of the current state of the technology and its limitations. This means staying up-to-date on the latest AI trends and developments, as well as investing in the necessary infrastructure and talent to support AI initiatives.

Another key aspect of strategic thinking in the age of AI is collaboration. CEOs must work closely with their teams to identify areas where AI can be most impactful and develop a roadmap for implementation. This requires a deep understanding of the organization's goals as well as the ability to communicate the potential benefits of AI to stakeholders across the company.

Moreover, strategic thinking requires CEOs to think beyond their own organization and consider how AI is transforming their industry as a whole. This means staying up-to-date on industry trends and disruptions and being prepared to pivot their strategy in response to changing market conditions.

Overall, the need for strategic thinking in the age of AI is critical for CEOs who want to stay ahead of the curve and drive business success. By developing a clear vision for how AI fits into their organization's overall strategy, staying up-to-date on the latest trends and developments, collaborating closely with their teams, and considering the bigger picture of their industry, CEOs can harness the power of AI to create a competitive advantage for their organization.

The importance of strategic thinking

Strategic thinking is crucial in an AI-driven world because it enables CEOs to see the big picture and identify opportunities and threats in a rapidly changing business landscape. With AI providing vast amounts of data and insights, CEOs need to be able to connect the dots and make strategic decisions that align with their organization's goals.

One way CEOs can develop their strategic thinking skills is by staying informed about emerging technologies and industry trends. They should also stay up-to-date with their competition and be aware of new entrants that may disrupt their industry. By understanding the market and the competitive landscape, CEOs can identify opportunities for growth and potential threats to their business.

Another way CEOs can develop their strategic thinking skills is by fostering a culture of innovation within their organization. They should encourage their employees to think outside the box and experiment with new ideas. By creating a safe space for creativity and risk-taking, CEOs can unlock new opportunities for growth and stay ahead of their competitors.

CEOs should also focus on developing a long-term vision for their organization. While AI can provide valuable insights for short-term decision-making, it is essential to consider the long-term implications of its strategic decisions. By having a clear vision and understanding of their organization's goals and values, CEOs can make strategic decisions that align with their overall mission.

Finally, CEOs can develop their strategic thinking skills by leveraging the power of AI itself. AI can provide valuable insights into market trends, customer behavior, and industry developments, which can help CEOs make more informed decisions. However, it is important to remember that AI is a tool, and CEOs must use their judgment and expertise to make the final decision.

In conclusion, strategic thinking is essential for CEOs to succeed in an AI-driven world. By staying informed, fostering innovation, developing a long-term vision, and leveraging the power of AI, CEOs can make strategic decisions that drive business success and keep them ahead of their competitors.

The Importance of Leadership in an AI-driven World

In an AI-driven world, the importance of leadership cannot be overstated. As organizations increasingly rely on AI to make decisions, it is the CEO's role to ensure that AI is being used effectively and ethically to drive business success. This chapter will explore the key competencies that CEOs need to develop to lead effectively in an AI-driven world.

One of the most critical competencies for CEOs is the ability to navigate the complex ethical considerations that arise with the implementation of AI. As AI is used to make decisions that can have a profound impact on individuals and society as a whole, CEOs need to ensure that ethical principles are integrated into the development and deployment of AI systems. This requires a deep understanding of ethical principles and a commitment to upholding them even in the face of difficult decisions.

Another crucial competency for CEOs in an AI-driven world is the ability to create a culture that embraces innovation while also fostering a sense of responsibility and accountability. Innovation is essential for organizations to remain competitive in a rapidly evolving landscape, but it must be balanced with a commitment to ethical and responsible practices. CEOs must encourage their teams to experiment and take risks while also ensuring that the organization is operating within legal and ethical boundaries.

Leadership in an AI-driven world also requires CEOs to have a deep understanding of the capabilities and limitations of AI. While AI can be a powerful tool for decision-making, it is not a panacea for all organizational challenges. CEOs need to be able to identify the areas where AI can provide the most significant benefits and those where human judgment and intuition are still essential. This requires a nuanced understanding of both AI and the organization's specific needs and goals.

AI implementation presents both potential benefits and challenges for CEOs. On the one hand, AI can enhance efficiency, accuracy, and productivity, leading to cost savings, increased revenue, and a competitive advantage. AI can automate mundane tasks, allowing employees to focus on higher-level tasks that require human judgment and creativity. AI can also provide insights that may not be readily apparent to humans, enabling organizations to make more informed decisions.

However, there are also challenges associated with integrating AI into existing business processes and systems. One significant challenge is data privacy and security. With the large amounts of data required for AI, there is an increased risk of data breaches and cyberattacks. It is essential for CEOs to prioritize data security and ensure that proper measures are in place to protect sensitive information.

Another challenge is the potential for AI to replace human jobs. While AI can automate certain tasks, it is not a replacement for human creativity and critical thinking. CEOs need to be aware of the impact of AI on their workforce and take measures to reskill and upskill employees to adapt to new roles and responsibilities in an AI-driven world.

Furthermore, implementing AI requires a significant investment in terms of time, resources, and expertise. Organizations need to have a clear strategy for AI implementation and ensure that they have the necessary resources and expertise to execute it effectively.

Even though AI presents numerous benefits for CEOs, such as enhanced efficiency, accuracy, and productivity, there are also challenges associated with its implementation. CEOs need to be aware of these challenges and take measures to address them, including prioritizing data security, re-skilling and up-skilling employees, and developing a clear strategy for AI implementation.

CEOs Must Communicate Effectively

Finally, CEOs need to be able to communicate effectively with all stakeholders about the role of AI in the organization. This includes communicating the benefits and potential risks of AI to employees, shareholders, customers, and the broader public. Effective communication is essential for building trust and ensuring that everyone understands the organization's commitment to ethical and responsible AI practices.

In order to lead effectively in an AI-driven environment, CEOs need to develop several key competencies:

1. Data literacy: As discussed earlier, data literacy is essential for CEOs to make informed decisions based on data-driven insights. They need to be able to understand and interpret data, identify patterns and trends, and use this information to drive business strategy.

2. Technological Savvy: CEOs need to have a basic understanding of the technologies underpinning AI, such as machine learning and natural language processing. This will enable them to better assess the potential of AI for their organization, identify opportunities for innovation, and communicate effectively with their technology teams.

3. Strategic Thinking: With the rise of AI, CEOs need to think more strategically about how to leverage this technology to drive business success. They need to be able to identify new markets and opportunities, set priorities, allocate resources, and make trade-offs in a fast-changing environment.

4. Change Management: Implementing AI can be a complex and challenging process, requiring significant changes to existing business processes and systems. CEOs need to be skilled in change management, communicating the benefits of AI to employees, and managing resistance to change.

5. Innovation and experimentation: Finally, CEOs need to foster a culture of innovation and experimentation in their organizations. This means encouraging employees to test new ideas, take calculated risks, and be open to failure as part of the learning process.

To develop these competencies, CEOs can take several steps:

Invest in training and education programs for themselves and their employees, focused on data literacy, technological savvy, and innovation.

Hire or appoint a Chief Data Officer or Chief Technology Officer to lead AI initiatives and provide strategic guidance to the CEO and senior leadership team.

Build cross-functional teams comprising business, technology, and data experts to work together on AI initiatives.

Encourage experimentation and risk-taking by creating a safe environment for employees to test new ideas and learn from failures.

Recognize and reward innovation by creating incentives for employees to develop and implement AI-based solutions.

In conclusion, leadership is essential in an AI-driven world, and CEOs must develop the competencies necessary to lead effectively in this landscape. This includes navigating complex ethical considerations, fostering a culture of innovation and responsibility, understanding the capabilities and limitations of AI, and communicating effectively with all stakeholders. By developing these competencies, CEOs can ensure that their organizations are well-positioned to succeed in the age of AI.

3

Chapter: 3

The challenges and opportunities of Artificial intelligence (AI) implementation.

As AI becomes an increasingly important tool for business decision-making, organizations are faced with both challenges and opportunities when it comes to implementing this technology.

This chapter could explore these challenges and opportunities in depth and examine the ways in which CEOs can navigate them to drive successful AI adoption.

One of the primary challenges of AI implementation is the need for significant investment in infrastructure, talent, and resources. Implementing AI requires a significant amount of data processing power, specialized hardware and software, and skilled personnel to manage and analyze the data. Additionally, the implementation process itself can be complex and time-consuming, requiring organizations to carefully manage timelines and budgets to ensure a successful outcome.

Another challenge of AI implementation is the potential for bias in AI systems. If not carefully managed, AI systems can perpetuate existing biases and discrimination in decision-making, which can have significant negative consequences for both the organization and its stakeholders. CEOs must be aware of this risk and take proactive steps to mitigate it, such as developing ethical AI frameworks and regularly auditing AI systems for bias.

Despite these challenges, the opportunities presented by AI implementation are significant. AI can help organizations gain new insights into their customers, markets, and operations, leading to increased efficiency, productivity, and profitability. It can also enable more personalized customer experiences as well as more targeted and effective marketing and sales strategies.

To successfully implement AI, CEOs must be able to navigate these challenges while capitalizing on the opportunities presented by this technology. They must develop a deep understanding of AI and its potential applications within their organization and work closely with IT teams and data scientists to develop a clear implementation roadmap.

Additionally, CEOs must ensure that they have the necessary resources and talent in place to support AI adoption. This may include investing in training and development programs to upskill existing employees as well as recruiting new talent with expertise in AI and data analytics.

Finally, it is essential that CEOs prioritize ethical considerations in AI implementation, ensuring that AI systems are designed and used in ways that are consistent with their organization's values and broader societal expectations. By taking a thoughtful and strategic approach to AI implementation, CEOs can successfully leverage this technology to drive business success while also mitigating the risks and challenges that come with it.

Business Transformation By AI

AI is transforming the way businesses operate, and as a result, there are numerous opportunities for organizations to gain a competitive advantage by implementing AI. However, there are also many challenges that organizations need to overcome to fully realize the potential of AI. In this section, we will discuss the challenges and opportunities of AI implementation.

Opportunities for AI Implementation:

1.a. **Improved Efficiency and Productivity**: AI can automate routine and repetitive tasks, freeing up employees to focus on more strategic activities that require human judgment and creativity. This leads to increased efficiency and productivity, allowing businesses to accomplish more with the same resources.

Improved efficiency and productivity are two of the most significant advantages of implementing AI in the workplace. By automating routine and repetitive tasks, AI allows employees to focus on more strategic activities that require human judgment and creativity. This can lead to significant time savings and improved productivity for businesses of all sizes.

b. **AI can automate a wide range of tasks**: from data entry and analysis to customer service and supply chain management. For example, AI-powered chatbots can handle customer queries and complaints, freeing up customer service representatives to handle more complex issues that require human interaction. Similarly, AI-powered systems can analyze vast amounts of data and provide insights that would be impossible for humans to gather and analyze manually.

By automating these tasks, businesses can accomplish more with the same resources. This can lead to significant cost savings and improved profitability. For example, a business that automates its supply chain management processes can reduce errors, improve efficiency, and save money on inventory and logistics costs.

c. Improving Efficiency

In addition to improving efficiency and productivity, AI can also improve the quality of work. By automating routine tasks, AI can reduce errors and improve accuracy. This can lead to improved customer satisfaction, reduced waste, and better overall performance.

However, it is important to note that implementing AI can be challenging. Businesses must invest in the necessary infrastructure and expertise to ensure that the technology is implemented effectively. This includes investing in the right hardware and software, as well as hiring or training employees with the necessary expertise to manage and maintain the AI systems.

In conclusion, improved efficiency and productivity are two of the most significant benefits of implementing AI in the workplace. By automating routine tasks, businesses can free up employees to focus on more strategic activities that require human judgment and creativity. This can lead to significant time savings, improved quality of work, and cost savings for businesses of all sizes. However, businesses must invest in the necessary infrastructure and expertise to ensure that AI is implemented effectively and can deliver on its promise of improved efficiency and productivity.

2. Enhanced Decision-Making: AI can analyze vast amounts of data and provide insights that humans might miss, leading to better-informed and more accurate decision-making. This is particularly useful in industries such as finance, healthcare, and logistics, where decisions must be made quickly and accurately.

AI has the potential to transform decision-making processes across a wide range of industries. One of the most significant advantages of AI is its ability to analyze vast amounts of data and provide insights that humans might miss. This leads to better-informed and more accurate decision-making, particularly in industries where decisions must be made quickly and accurately, such as finance, healthcare, and logistics.

In the finance industry, for example, AI-powered systems can analyze vast amounts of financial data to identify trends and make predictions. This can help traders make more informed investment decisions and reduce the risk of financial losses. AI can also be used to monitor financial transactions and detect fraud, improving the accuracy and efficiency of fraud detection systems.

In the healthcare industry, AI can be used to analyze patient data and provide insights that can improve diagnosis and treatment. For example, AI-powered systems can analyze medical images to detect early signs of disease, improving the accuracy and efficiency of diagnostic processes. AI can also be used to monitor patients vital signs and detect early warning signs of complications, improving patient outcomes and reducing healthcare costs.

In the logistics industry, AI can be used to optimize supply chain processes and improve delivery times. For example, AI-powered systems can analyze shipping data to identify bottlenecks and inefficiencies in the supply chain, allowing businesses to make more informed decisions about inventory management and logistics. AI can also be used to optimize delivery routes and reduce transportation costs, improving efficiency and profitability.

Overall, AI has the potential to significantly enhance decision-making processes across a wide range of industries. By analyzing vast amounts of data and providing insights that humans might miss, AI can improve the accuracy and efficiency of decision-making processes, leading to better outcomes for businesses and consumers alike. However, it is important to ensure that AI systems are implemented in a responsible and ethical manner, taking into account potential biases and ensuring that decisions are transparent and explainable.

Another key advantage of AI in decision-making is its ability to learn and adapt over time. AI systems can be programmed to continuously learn from new data and adjust their algorithms accordingly, leading to improved accuracy and efficiency over time.

This is particularly useful in industries where data is constantly changing, such as finance and marketing. AI-powered systems can analyze customer data in real-time and make recommendations for personalized marketing campaigns, improving the effectiveness of marketing strategies and increasing customer engagement.

In addition, AI can help businesses identify and mitigate risks before they become major issues. By analyzing data from various sources, including social media and news outlets, AI can detect early warning signs of potential risks such as supply chain disruptions, cyberattacks, and reputational issues. This can help businesses make proactive decisions to mitigate these risks, reducing the impact on their operations and reputation.

However, implementing AI in decision-making processes also presents challenges. One of the main challenges is ensuring that the AI systems are transparent and explainable. This is particularly important in industries such as healthcare, where decisions can have life-or-death consequences. Businesses must ensure that the AI systems are transparent and explainable so that decisions can be easily understood and audited if necessary.

Note: Across a wide range of industries, AI has the potential to significantly improve decision-making processes. AI can enhance the accuracy, efficiency, and effectiveness of decision-making processes by analyzing enormous amounts of data, learning and adapting over time, and assisting businesses in identifying and mitigating risks. To guarantee that decisions are impartial and moral, businesses must guarantee that AI systems are transparent, explicable, and unbiased.

3. **Personalization**: AI can personalize customer experiences, leading to increased customer satisfaction and loyalty. For example, personalized recommendations based on a customer's past behavior can increase the likelihood of repeat business.

Personalization is a key advantage of AI in the business world, and it has the potential to significantly enhance the customer experience. By analyzing vast amounts of data, AI can personalize customer experiences and make recommendations based on a customer's past behavior, leading to increased customer satisfaction and loyalty.

One example of this is personalized recommendations in e-commerce. When a customer visits an e-commerce website, AI-powered systems can analyze their browsing and purchase histories to recommend products that they are more likely to be interested in. This not only saves the customer time and effort in searching for products, but it also increases the likelihood of repeat business and customer loyalty.

In addition, AI can personalize customer interactions in customer service. When a customer contacts a business with a question or issue,

AI-powered chat bots can analyze the customer's past interactions and provide personalized recommendations or solutions. This can help businesses resolve customer issues more quickly and efficiently, leading to increased customer satisfaction and loyalty.

AI can also personalize marketing campaigns, tailoring messages and offers to specific customer segments based on their past behavior and preferences. This can increase the effectiveness of marketing campaigns, leading to higher engagement and conversion rates.

One of the key advantages of AI-powered personalization is its ability to analyze vast amounts of data in real-time. This means that AI can make personalized recommendations and tailor customer interactions in a matter of seconds, leading to a more seamless and efficient customer experience. For example, an AI-powered chatbot can analyze a customer's past interactions with a business and provide personalized recommendations or solutions to their questions or issues, leading to a faster and more effective resolution of the problem.

Another advantage of AI-powered personalization is its ability to adapt and learn over time. As AI systems analyze more data and make more personalized recommendations, they become better at predicting customer preferences and behavior. This leads to more accurate and effective personalization, which can significantly enhance the customer experience and increase customer satisfaction and loyalty.

Moreover, AI can personalize the customer experience across multiple channels, including social media, email, and mobile devices. This enables businesses to provide a consistent and personalized experience to customers, regardless of the channel they are using. For example, an e-commerce business can use AI to provide personalized product recommendations to a customer through their mobile device, email, or social media, leading to a more seamless and convenient shopping experience.

AI-powered personalization has the potential to significantly enhance the customer experience and increase customer satisfaction and loyalty. By analyzing vast amounts of data in real-time, adapting and learning over time, and personalizing customer interactions across multiple channels, AI can provide a more seamless and efficient customer experience.

4. Cost Savings: AI can reduce costs by automating tasks that would otherwise require manual labor, reducing errors, and improving efficiency.

Cost savings are another significant advantage of AI implementation in business. AI can help reduce costs by automating tasks that would otherwise require manual labor, reducing errors, and improving efficiency.

One of the ways that AI can help reduce costs is through automation. By automating routine and repetitive tasks, businesses can reduce the need for manual labor, leading to savings on salaries and benefits. For example, AI-powered systems can automate data entry, customer service inquiries, and other administrative tasks, reducing the need for human intervention and freeing up employees to focus on more strategic activities.

In addition, AI can help reduce errors in business processes, leading to cost savings through improved accuracy and efficiency. For example, AI can be used to analyze data and identify patterns and anomalies that humans might miss, reducing the likelihood of errors in decision-making. Moreover, AI-powered systems can monitor business processes in real-time, identifying potential issues before they become significant problems and allowing businesses to take corrective action quickly.

AI can also aid in making business processes more efficient, which can reduce waste and increase productivity, resulting in cost savings. AI can, for instance, be applied to supply chain logistics optimization to cut down on the time and expense associated with distribution, storage, and transportation. Aside from analyzing customer data to find trends and preferences, AI-powered systems can also help businesses better target their marketing initiatives and product offerings at particular customer segments, resulting in greater success.

Despite the potential cost-saving benefits of AI, there are also implementation costs to consider. Implementing AI-powered systems can require significant investments in technology, training, and infrastructure. Therefore, businesses must carefully consider the costs and benefits of AI implementation before deciding to invest.

As a result of automation, a decline in errors, and increased productivity, AI can help businesses cut costs. AI can help businesses save a lot of money by automating repetitive and routine tasks, decreasing decision-making errors, and enhancing business process efficiency. However, before deciding to invest in this technology, businesses must carefully consider the implementation costs of AI.

5. **Competitive Advantage:** AI can provide businesses with a competitive advantage by enabling them to make faster and more accurate decisions, offer more personalized experiences, and reduce costs.

One of the significant advantages of AI implementation in business is that it can provide businesses with a competitive edge. AI can enable businesses to make faster and more accurate decisions, offer more personalized experiences, and reduce costs, all of which can lead to a competitive advantage.

By providing businesses with faster and more accurate decision-making capabilities, AI can enable businesses to stay ahead of their competitors. For example, in the finance industry, AI-powered systems can analyze vast amounts of data in real-time to identify market trends and make predictions about future market movements. This information can be used to make informed investment decisions and gain a competitive advantage over other firms.

Moreover, AI can enable businesses to offer more personalized experiences to their customers, which can lead to increased customer satisfaction and loyalty. By analyzing customer data and behavior, AI-powered systems can provide personalized recommendations and tailored marketing campaigns that are more likely to resonate with individual customers. This can give businesses an advantage over their competitors, who may not be using AI to provide personalized experiences.

Furthermore, AI can help businesses reduce costs, which can provide a competitive advantage by allowing them to offer more competitive pricing or invest more in other areas of their business. By automating routine tasks and improving efficiency in business processes, AI can help businesses reduce costs and improve their bottom line. This can enable them to offer lower prices than their competitors or invest more in research and development to create innovative new products or services.

AI can provide businesses with a competitive advantage by enabling faster and more accurate decision-making, offering more personalized experiences to customers, and reducing costs. By leveraging the power of AI, businesses can stay ahead of their competitors and create new opportunities for growth and success. However, it is essential to note that implementing AI requires careful planning and investment, and businesses must carefully weigh the costs and benefits before deciding to invest in this technology.

Challenges of AI Implementation:

1. **Data Quality and Bias:** AI algorithms are only as good as the data they are trained on, and if the data is biased or of poor quality, it can lead to inaccurate predictions or decisions. It is important to ensure that the data used to train AI algorithms is of high quality and free from bias.

While AI has the potential to provide businesses with a competitive advantage, it is important to note that AI algorithms are only as good as the data they are trained on. If the data used to train the AI algorithm is biased or of poor quality, it can lead to inaccurate predictions or decisions. This is where the issue of data quality and bias comes in.

Data Quality: For AI algorithms to produce accurate results, they need to be trained on high quality data. This means that the data used to train the AI algorithm needs to be accurate, complete, and representative of the problem at hand. If the data used to train the AI algorithm is incomplete or inaccurate, it can lead to incorrect predictions or decisions. For example, if a company is using AI to predict customer behavior, but the data used to train the AI algorithm is incomplete or inaccurate, it can lead to incorrect predictions, resulting in lost sales and dissatisfied customers.

Data bias is another challenge that businesses need to address when implementing AI. Bias can occur when the data used to train the AI algorithm is not representative of the population it is supposed to predict. For example, if a company is using AI to predict loan eligibility, but the data used to train the AI algorithm is biased towards certain demographics, it can lead to discriminatory loan decisions. This can damage the reputation of the company and lead to legal repercussions.

To ensure that the data used to train AI algorithms is of high quality and free from bias, businesses need to invest in data cleaning and preparation. This involves identifying and addressing any errors, inconsistencies, or biases in the data set before it is used to train the AI algorithm. Additionally, businesses can use diverse data sources to ensure that the data set used to train the AI algorithm is representative of the population it is supposed to predict.

While AI can provide businesses with a competitive advantage, it is important to ensure that the data used to train AI algorithms is of high quality and free from bias. By addressing these challenges, businesses can ensure that their AI algorithms produce accurate and reliable results, leading to better decision-making and increased competitiveness.

Prioritizing data bias and ensuring data quality are essential steps in implementing AI for businesses.

By doing this, businesses can make sure that the results produced by their AI algorithms are accurate and trustworthy, which can improve decision-making and boost competitiveness. It is crucial to remember that bias and poor data quality are ongoing issues that businesses must deal with. Businesses must regularly review and update their data sets in order to make sure that their AI algorithms are accurate and unbiased as new data becomes available or as the population being predicted changes.

To address these issues, businesses also need a diverse team working on their AI implementation. This includes experts in ethics, diversity, and inclusion in addition to data scientists. Businesses can make sure they are considering different perspectives and addressing potential biases in their data sets by assembling a diverse team to work on AI implementation.

In conclusion, while AI has the potential to give businesses a competitive edge, it is critical to address issues with data quality and bias to make sure that the outcomes produced by AI algorithms are accurate, dependable, and unbiased. Businesses can do this to improve their decision-making processes and gain a competitive edge in their particular industries.

2. Lack of Expertise: AI is a complex field, and there is a shortage of experts who understand the technology and can implement it effectively. Businesses must invest in training and development to build a workforce with the necessary expertise.

Yes, a lack of expertise is a major challenge for businesses looking to implement AI technology. AI is a complex field that requires expertise in multiple areas, such as data science, computer programming, and machine learning. Moreover, AI technology is rapidly evolving, which means that businesses need to continuously train their workforce to stay up-to-date with the latest developments.

However, there is currently a shortage of experts who understand AI technology and can effectively implement it in a business context. This shortage is especially acute in certain areas, such as natural language processing and computer vision. As a result, businesses may struggle to find qualified personnel to lead their AI initiatives.

To address this challenge, businesses must invest in training and development to build a workforce with the necessary expertise. This can include providing training programs for existing employees or partnering with universities and other institutions to recruit new talent. Additionally, businesses may consider outsourcing some of their AI-related tasks to external service providers who have the necessary expertise.

It is important to note that building expertise in AI is a long-term investment. Businesses should not expect immediate results but instead focus on building a strong foundation of expertise that can be leveraged over time. By investing in training and development, businesses can build a workforce that is equipped to effectively implement and manage AI technology, leading to improved decision-making, increased efficiency, and a competitive advantage in the marketplace.

Lack of expertise in AI is a significant challenge for businesses in all industries, as AI is becoming increasingly important in driving digital transformation and competitiveness. The demand for AI expertise has far outpaced the supply of skilled professionals, creating a talent gap that businesses are struggling to fill. The lack of expertise in AI is particularly acute in smaller businesses, where resources may be limited and it may be difficult to attract and retain top talent.

One approach to overcoming the lack of expertise in AI is to invest in training and development programs that can build a workforce with the necessary skills. These programs can range from basic training in data science and machine learning to advanced programs that cover more complex topics like deep learning and neural networks. Additionally, businesses can partner with universities, research institutions, and other organizations to identify and recruit talent with the right skillsets.

Another option is to outsource AI-related tasks to external service providers who have the necessary expertise.

This approach can be especially helpful for smaller businesses that may not have the resources to build an in-house team. Outsourcing AI tasks can also allow businesses to access cutting-edge technology and expertise without making a long-term commitment.

In addition to investing in talent and outsourcing, businesses can also explore alternative AI technologies that require less expertise. For example, many cloud-based AI platforms offer pre-built models that can be easily integrated into existing systems without requiring advanced knowledge of AI.

It is critical to understand that developing AI expertise is a continuous process. Businesses must be ready to adapt to changing technology and keep up with the most recent advancements. Businesses can build a solid foundation of expertise that can be used over time to drive digital transformation, improve decision-making, and gain a competitive advantage in the marketplace by investing in talent development, outsourcing, and alternative AI technologies.

3. **Integration with Legacy Systems:** Implementing AI can be challenging if existing systems are not designed to work with the technology. Businesses must invest in the necessary infrastructure to ensure that AI can be integrated effectively.

The integration of AI with legacy systems can be a significant challenge for businesses. Many existing systems were not designed to work with the latest AI technologies, and integrating them can be time-consuming and expensive. However, it is essential to integrate AI effectively to ensure that businesses can leverage its benefits fully.

One of the main challenges of integrating AI with legacy systems is the need to ensure that the new technology works seamlessly with existing processes. This requires a deep understanding of both the legacy systems and the new AI technologies, as well as expertise in software engineering and system integration. In some cases, it may be necessary to re-engineer existing processes to accommodate AI effectively.

Another challenge is the need to ensure that data can be accessed and shared effectively between the legacy systems and the new AI technologies. This requires careful planning and coordination to ensure that the data is available in the right format and that it can be processed and analyzed effectively. In some cases, it may be necessary to migrate data to a new platform or restructure existing data to ensure compatibility.

In addition to the technical challenges, there may also be cultural and organizational barriers to integrating AI with legacy systems. Employees may be resistant to change or lack the necessary skills and expertise to work effectively with new technologies. Businesses must invest in training and development to ensure that employees have the necessary skills to work with AI and can effectively integrate it into their workflows.

Integrating AI with legacy systems can also pose challenges related to data management and security. In some cases, legacy systems may use outdated data formats or lack the necessary security protocols to protect sensitive data. This can make it difficult to effectively integrate AI without compromising data integrity or security.

To address these challenges, businesses may need to invest in updating legacy systems to ensure compatibility with AI technology. This may involve upgrading hardware, software, or network infrastructure to meet the requirements of AI algorithms. It may also involve implementing new data management and security protocols to ensure that data is properly managed and protected.

In addition to these technical challenges, there may also be cultural or organizational barriers to integrating AI with legacy systems. Some employees may be resistant to change or may lack the necessary skills or knowledge to effectively utilize AI technology. Addressing these challenges may require investing in training and development programs to build a culture of innovation and prepare employees for the future of work.

Despite the challenges, integrating AI with legacy systems can provide significant benefits to businesses. By leveraging the latest AI technologies, businesses can automate routine tasks, reduce errors, and improve efficiency, leading to cost savings and increased productivity. Additionally, AI can provide new insights and data-driven recommendations, enabling businesses to make better-informed decisions and gain a competitive advantage in their industries.

4. **Change Management:** Implementing AI often requires significant changes to organizational processes and culture, which can be difficult to manage. Businesses must invest in change management to ensure that employees are prepared for the changes and can adapt effectively.

Implementing AI in a business can be a disruptive process that requires significant changes to existing processes and workflows. This can create resistance from employees who may be reluctant to embrace new technology or fear that their jobs will be replaced by automation. To successfully implement AI, businesses must invest in change management to ensure that employees are prepared for the changes and can adapt effectively.

Change management involves a structured approach to transitioning individuals, teams, and organizations from their current state to a desired future state. This can include communication and education campaigns to help employees understand the benefits of AI and how it will impact their roles. It also involves identifying and addressing any concerns or resistance from employees and providing support to help them adapt to new ways of working.

Effective change management can also involve involving employees in the AI implementation process. This can include soliciting feedback from employees on potential AI use cases and involving them in testing and piloting new AI systems. By involving employees in the process, businesses can build buy-in and support for the technology, reducing resistance and increasing the likelihood of successful implementation.

Change management is an important aspect of successful AI implementation because it requires a significant shift in organizational culture and processes. It is essential to involve employees in the process of implementing AI and to communicate with them effectively to ensure their buy-in and support. Businesses must also invest in training and development to help employees adapt to the new technology and acquire the necessary skills to work effectively with it.

Another important aspect of change management is addressing any resistance to change. Employees may be hesitant to embrace AI if they perceive it as a threat to their jobs or if they feel that they do not have the necessary skills to work with the technology. Businesses must address these concerns proactively and provide employees with the necessary support and resources to adapt to the changes.

Businesses must also be open and honest about how AI is affecting the workforce. While AI can increase productivity and efficiency, it can occasionally result in job displacement as well. Businesses should have a strategy in place to handle these changes and support any affected employees. In conclusion, effective change management is essential for the implementation of AI. Businesses can increase the acceptance and success of the technology by making an investment in change management, which will ensure that their employees are ready for the changes and can adapt successfully.

In conclusion, the challenges and opportunities of AI implementation are significant. Businesses that invest in the necessary infrastructure, expertise, and change management can reap the benefits of AI, including increased efficiency, productivity, and competitiveness. However, businesses must also address the challenges of data quality, bias, ethics, integration, and change management to ensure that the benefits of AI are realized without compromising ethical standards.

4

Chapter: 4

The Future of Retail

How artificial intelligence (AI) and Automation are Disrupting the Customer Experience"

The retail industry has undergone a significant transformation over the last decade, with the advent of new technologies and the rise of e-commerce fundamentally changing the way that customers shop. One of the most significant developments in this space has been the increased adoption of AI and automation to improve the customer experience, streamline operations, and increase efficiency. This chapter will examine the ways in which AI is transforming the retail industry, with a particular focus on personalized recommendations, chat-bots, inventory management, robotics, and cashier-less checkout. We will also explore some of the potential benefits and challenges associated with these technologies and consider what the future of retail might look like in an era of rapid technological change.

The use of AI and automation in the retail industry is becoming increasingly prevalent, with retailers leveraging these technologies to enhance the customer experience and remain competitive in a rapidly evolving market. Personalized recommendations, for exam-

49

ple, are powered by sophisticated algorithms that analyze customer data to provide tailored product suggestions, while chat-bots and virtual assistants offer 24/7 customer service that can answer questions and resolve issues in real-time.

AI-powered inventory management systems also help retailers optimize their supply chains and reduce waste by predicting demand and automating orders. Robotics and automation, on the other hand, are being used to improve order fulfillment processes, with robots assisting with tasks such as picking, packing, and shipping. And the concept of cashier-less checkout, made possible by AI and automation, is being increasingly explored, with retailers leveraging these technologies to enable customers to simply walk in, grab what they need, and walk out without the need for a checkout process.

In addition, robotics and automation are being used to improve order fulfillment processes, with robots assisting with tasks such as picking, packing, and shipping. This helps retailers improve their operational efficiency and reduce costs.

And augmented reality and facial recognition are being used to enhance customer engagement and offer a more immersive shopping experience. Retailers can use these technologies to offer virtual try on experiences or personalized product recommendations based on a customer's facial features.

The use of robotics and automation in the retail industry is revolutionizing the way that order fulfillment processes are handled. Retailers are increasingly turning to these technologies to improve efficiency and accuracy in their warehouses and to meet the demands of today's fast-paced e-commerce market.

One of the primary areas where robotics and automation are being used is in the picking, packing, and shipping of orders. Traditionally, these tasks were carried out by human workers, but the use of robots and automation systems is allowing retailers to handle a much larger volume of orders with greater speed and accuracy.

Robotic systems for order fulfillment typically use a combination of sensors, cameras, and algorithms to navigate warehouses and locate products. Once a product is identified, robots can pick it up and transport it to a designated packing station, where it is prepared for shipping. Robots can work alongside human workers in warehouses, helping to improve efficiency and reduce the risk of injury or strain.

One example of a company using robotics and automation in order fulfillment is Amazon. The company has been using robots in its fulfillment centers for several years, with robots carrying out tasks such as moving inventory and transporting packages. According to Amazon, these systems have helped to reduce operating costs and increase efficiency in their warehouses.

Ocado, a UK-based online grocer, is another business that uses robotic systems for order fulfillment. Robotic pickers and conveyors are used by Ocado to move goods through its warehouses and get orders ready for delivery. The business asserts that by using robotics and automation, it has been able to process orders with greater accuracy and efficiency than would be possible using only human workers. While there are many advantages to using automation and robotics for order fulfillment, there are some drawbacks as well. As more tasks are automated, there may be worries about job displacement as well as high implementation costs for these systems. Additionally, there is a need for skilled workers to maintain and operate these systems, which may require additional training or hiring.

Despite these difficulties, retailers will probably continue to use automation and robotics to fill orders as they try to keep up with the needs of the e-commerce market. Retailers can increase productivity, cut costs, and give customers a better overall experience by using these technologies.

In addition to the use of robotics and automation for order fulfillment, retailers are also turning to AI to enhance the in-store shopping experience. By leveraging technologies such as augmented reality and facial recognition, retailers are able to provide customers with personalized, engaging experiences that can help drive sales and build brand loyalty.

One way that retailers are using AI to enhance the in-store experience is through the use of augmented reality (AR). AR technology allows customers to virtually try on products or visualize how they might look in their homes before making a purchase. For example, a customer might use an AR app to see how a piece of furniture would look in their living room or to try on virtual clothing items to see how they fit and look. This technology can help increase customer engagement and improve the overall shopping experience.

Facial recognition technology is another way that retailers are using AI to enhance the in-store experience. By using cameras and algorithms to identify individual customers, retailers can provide personalized recommendations and offers based on a customer's past purchase history or preferences. For example, a customer might receive a special offer or discount when they enter the store based on their past purchases or browsing history. This technology can help build customer loyalty and drive sales.

However, the use of facial recognition technology has also raised concerns about privacy and security. Retailers must be careful to ensure that they are using this technology in a responsible and ethical manner and that they are transparent about how they are collecting and using customer data.

AI and automation are enabling retailers to gather and analyze enormous amounts of data on consumer behavior in addition to enhancing the customer experience. Retailers can gain insights into customer preferences and purchasing patterns by utilizing technologies like machine learning and data analytics. These insights can then be used to guide product development and marketing strategies.

Using sensors and smart devices in stores is one way retailers are using AI and automation to gather and analyze customer data. These gadgets can monitor a customer's movements and behavior, including the products they look at and the length of time they spend in various store locations. This information can be used to personalize marketing offers and messages, as well as optimize store layouts and product placement.

Online retailers are also using AI and automation to collect and analyze customer data. By tracking customer interactions with their websites and apps, retailers can gain insights into customer preferences and behavior, such as which products they search for or how they navigate the site. This data can be used to create personalized product recommendations and targeted marketing messages.

Machine learning algorithms are also being used to analyze customer data in order to identify patterns and trends. For example, a retailer might use machine learning to identify which products are frequently purchased together or to predict which customers are most likely to make a purchase. This information can be used to inform product development and marketing strategies, as well as to improve supply chain management and inventory forecasting.

Retailers are now able to gather and analyze enormous amounts of data on customer behavior thanks to the use of AI and automation in the sector. Retailers can learn more about consumer preferences and purchasing patterns by utilizing these technologies, which can then be applied to product development, marketing plans, and other areas. However, it is crucial that retailers exercise caution when gathering and using customer data, taking precautions to make sure they are doing so in a responsible and ethical manner.

While the use of AI and automation in the retail industry has the potential to revolutionize the way that retailers engage with customers and manage their operations, it also raises concerns about job displacement and the need for re-skilling and up-skilling workers to adapt to the changing landscape.

As more retailers turn to robotics and automation for tasks such as order fulfillment and inventory management, there is a concern that traditional retail jobs may become obsolete. For example, the use of self-checkout machines and automated kiosks may reduce the need for human cashiers and customer service representatives. This could result in job losses and the need for workers to reskill or up-skill in order to stay relevant in the industry.

However, some experts argue that the use of AI and automation may actually create new job opportunities in the retail industry. For example, the development and maintenance of these technologies require skilled workers in areas such as software development and data analytics. Additionally, as retailers shift their focus toward providing personalized customer experiences, there may be an increased demand for workers with skills in areas such as customer service and marketing.

Retailers must invest in re-skilling and up-skilling programs for their staff in order to reduce the potential negative effects of AI and automation on the retail workforce. In a changing industry, this can help employees gain new skills and maintain their relevance. The need for social safety nets and programs to assist workers who are displaced by technological advancements may also need to be taken into account by policymakers.

The use of AI and automation in the retail sector has the potential to completely change how retailers interact with their customers and run their businesses, but it is important to take into account the potential effects on the workforce. Retailers can support the preparation of their employees for the industry's changing landscape by investing in re-skilling and up-skilling programs for them.

Overall, the use of AI in the retail industry is transforming the way that retailers engage with customers, both online and in-store. By leveraging technologies such as AR and facial recognition, retailers can provide personalized, engaging experiences that can help build customer loyalty and drive sales. However, it is important that retailers approach these technologies with caution, taking steps to ensure that they are using them in a responsible and ethical manner.

While the application of AI and automation in the retail sector has the potential to revolutionize the sector, it also raises questions about job displacement and the requirement for workers to acquire new skills to keep up with the changing environment.

Finally there is no denying that automation and AI are revolutionizing the retail sector and influencing how consumers shop both in-person and online. In-depth discussion of these trends and predictions about the state of retail in an era of rapid technological change are provided in this chapter.

Recap:

1. AI and automation are increasingly being used in the retail industry to improve the customer experience, streamline operations, and increase efficiency.
2. Personalized recommendations powered by AI algorithms are becoming more prevalent, with retailers leveraging customer data to offer tailored product suggestions.
3. Chat-bots and virtual assistants are being used to provide customer service, answering questions and resolving issues in real-time.
4. AI-powered inventory management systems are helping retailers optimize their supply chains and reduce waste by predicting demand and automating orders.
5. Robotics and automation are being used to improve order fulfillment processes, with robots assisting with tasks such as picking, packing, and shipping.
6. The concept of cashier-less checkout is being increasingly explored, with retailers leveraging AI and automation to enable customers to simply walk in, grab what they need, and walk out without the need for a checkout process.
7. AI is also being used to improve in-store experiences, with retailers leveraging technologies such as AR and facial recognition to enhance customer engagement.
8. The rise of e-commerce and online marketplaces has made it easier for retailers to leverage AI and automation to improve the customer experience, with many online retailers utilizing personalized recommendations and chat-bots to provide a seamless shopping experience.

9. AI and automation are also enabling retailers to collect and analyze vast amounts of data on customer behavior, which can be used to make informed decisions about product development, marketing strategies, and more.

10. While the use of AI and automation in retail has the potential to revolutionize the industry, it also raises concerns about job displacement and the need for re-skilling and up-skilling workers to adapt to the changing landscapes.

5

Chapter: 5

The future of the C-suite

The future of the C-suite in a world where machines are increasingly taking on decision-making roles

The future C-suite will undoubtedly look very different from the one we have today as the use of artificial intelligence (AI) and machine learning (ML) increases. Senior executives will need to develop new skills and expertise to keep up with the changing business environment as machines assume more and more decision-making roles. In this article, we'll look at a few of the ways that the C-suite will probably change as AI becomes more commonplace, as well as the effects of those changes on businesses and society at large.

The increased use of data-driven decision-making is one of the biggest changes we can anticipate. Machines will be able to spot patterns and trends that human decision-makers might not notice because they can analyze massive amounts of data in real time. Companies will be able to make better decisions and react to shifting market conditions more quickly as a result. However, this also means that in order for senior executives to make wise decisions, they will need to have a solid grasp of data analytics and be able to interpret the insights produced by machines.

Another important change will be the need for senior executives to be able to collaborate effectively with machines. This will require a different set of skills from those traditionally associated with C-suite roles. For example, executives will need to be able to communicate effectively with machines and understand the limitations and biases of the algorithms they are using. They will also need to be able to identify areas where machines can add value and work with data scientists and other experts to develop new applications of AI and ML.

The rise of AI in the C-suite also raises important ethical questions. As machines take on more decision-making roles, who will be responsible for the outcomes of those decisions? Will machines be held accountable for their actions, or will this responsibility fall to the humans who programmed them? These are complex issues that will need to be addressed by businesses and society as a whole.

Another important consideration is the impact of AI on the workforce. As machines take on more decision-making roles, it is likely that some jobs will be automated, leading to job losses in certain industries. This will require companies and governments to invest in retraining programs and other initiatives to support workers who are displaced by automation.

The future of the C-suite in a world where machines are increasingly taking on decision-making roles is of paramount importance for both the C-suite and organizations as a whole. Here are some reasons why:

1. **Maximizing the potential of AI and ML:** As machines become increasingly sophisticated in their ability to analyze vast amounts of data, organizations that do not adapt risk falling behind their competitors. The C-suite has a responsibility to ensure that their organization is leveraging AI and ML effectively in order to maximize their potential for growth and success.

2. **Maintaining a competitive edge:** Organizations that are slow to adapt to the changing landscape of decision-making risk losing their competitive edge in the marketplace. The C-suite must be prepared to lead their organizations through this technological shift and ensure that they are staying ahead of the curve.

3. **Ensuring ethical decision-making:** As machines take on decision-making roles, there are significant ethical considerations that must be taken into account. The C-suite has a responsibility to ensure that the use of AI and ML is guided by ethical principles and that they are taking steps to mitigate any potential negative impacts.

4. **Managing the impact on the workforce:** The rise of AI and ML in decision-making roles has the potential to impact the workforce in significant ways, including job loss due to automation. The C-suite must be prepared to manage this impact by investing in retraining programs and other support initiatives.

5. **Leading teams that include both humans and machines:** The C-suite must be prepared to lead teams that include both humans and machines and to ensure effective collaboration between the two. This requires new leadership skills and an openness to new technologies and ways of working.

The future of the C-suite in a world where machines are increasingly taking on decision-making roles is critically important for organizations to remain competitive, make ethical decisions, and manage the impact on their workforce. The C-suite must be prepared to lead its organizations through this technological shift in a way that benefits everyone.

Collaboration between humans and machines

Effective collaboration between humans and machines is crucial in a world where machines are increasingly taking on decision-making roles. Here are some reasons why:

1. **Machines can augment human decision-making:** Machines can process vast amounts of data quickly and accurately, which can augment human decision-making by providing valuable insights and predictions. By collaborating effectively, humans and machines can work together to make better decisions than either could alone,

Machines can play a crucial role in augmenting human decision-making in many industries and fields. By processing vast amounts of data, machines can provide valuable insights and predictions that humans may not be able to see. For example, in finance, ML algorithms can analyze financial data and identify patterns that may not be apparent to human analysts, helping to inform investment decisions.

In healthcare, ML algorithms can analyze vast amounts of patient data to identify risk factors for certain diseases and predict which patients are most likely to benefit from specific treatments. This can help doctors and healthcare providers make better decisions about patient care, leading to improved health outcomes.

By collaborating effectively with machines, humans can leverage these insights to make better decisions than they could alone. For example, in manufacturing, ML algorithms can analyze data from sensors and other sources to optimize production processes and reduce waste. By working together with machines, human operators can use this data to make real time decisions that improve efficiency and reduce costs.

However, it is important to note that effective collaboration between humans and machines requires more than simply using machines to process data. Humans must also be able to interpret the insights provided by machines and use them to inform their decision-making. This requires a combination of technical skills, such as data analysis and ML, as well as critical thinking and problem-solving skills.

Additionally, effective collaboration between humans and machines also requires trust. Humans must be able to trust the insights provided by machines, and machines must be designed to be transparent and explainable so that humans can understand how they arrived at their predictions and recommendations.

In general, the automation of human decision-making has the potential to revolutionize many fields and industries, resulting in better outcomes and increased effectiveness. To realize these advantages, however, human and machine interaction must be effective.

2. **Human input is essential for ethical decision-making.** While machines can provide valuable data-driven insights, humans are needed to provide context and make ethical judgments. Effective collaboration between humans and machines can ensure that ethical considerations are taken into account in decision-making.

While machines can provide valuable data-driven insights, they lack the ability to make ethical judgments on their own. Ethical considerations are critical in decision-making, particularly in fields such as healthcare, finance, and law. These decisions often have significant impacts on individuals and society as a whole, and it is important to ensure that they are made in an ethical and responsible manner.

This is where human input becomes essential. Humans have the ability to provide context and make ethical judgments based on their own experiences, values, and beliefs. This allows them to consider a range of factors beyond just the data and weigh the potential benefits and harms of different decisions. For example, in healthcare, ethical considerations may include considerations of patient privacy, informed consent, and patient autonomy, among others.

Effective collaboration between humans and machines can ensure that ethical considerations are taken into account in decision-making. For example, in finance, ML algorithms can analyze vast amounts of financial data to identify potential investment opportunities. However, human investment managers are still needed to make ethical judgments about whether these investments align with their client's values and goals.

Similarly, in healthcare, ML algorithms can help identify potential treatment options for patients based on their medical histories and other data. However, doctors and healthcare providers are still needed to make ethical judgments about the risks and benefits of different treatment options, as well as other considerations such as patient preferences and quality of life.

Effective collaboration between humans and machines requires that humans have the necessary knowledge and skills to interpret the insights provided by machines and to make ethical judgments based on that information. It also requires that machines be transparent and explainable so that humans can understand how they arrived at their predictions and recommendations.

While machines can provide valuable data-driven insights, human input is essential for ethical decision-making. Effective collaboration between humans and machines can ensure that ethical considerations are taken into account in decision-making, leading to better outcomes and greater trust in the decision-making process.

3. **Human creativity is still necessary:** While machines can analyze data and identify patterns, they lack the creativity and intuition of human beings. Effective collaboration between humans and machines can ensure that both data-driven insights and human creativity are taken into account in decision-making.

Human creativity is a crucial aspect of decision-making, particularly in areas that require innovation and problem-solving. While machines can analyze vast amounts of data and identify patterns, they lack the creativity and intuition that humans possess. For example, in fields such as art, music, and design, human creativity is essential for producing unique and innovative works.

In decision-making, human creativity is also necessary for identifying new opportunities and solutions to complex problems. Humans have the ability to think outside the box and to come up with new and innovative ideas that may not be immediately apparent from the data. For example, in business, human creativity may be needed to identify new markets, develop new products or services, and create effective marketing strategies.

Effective collaboration between humans and machines can ensure that both data-driven insights and human creativity are taken into account in decision-making. By leveraging the strengths of both humans and machines, organizations can make better decisions and achieve better outcomes. For example, in the field of product design, machines can generate design options based on user data and preferences, while human designers can use their creativity and intuition to refine those options and come up with new and innovative solutions.

In addition, effective collaboration between humans and machines can lead to more diverse and inclusive decision-making. Machines are trained on existing data, which may contain biases and limitations. By incorporating human input and creativity into the decision-making process, organizations can ensure that a broader range of perspectives and experiences are taken into account.

However, effective collaboration between humans and machines requires that humans have the necessary skills and training to work effectively with machines. This includes skills such as data analysis, programming, and critical thinking. It also requires that machines be designed to be user-friendly and accessible so that humans can easily interpret the insights provided by machines and incorporate them into their decision-making.

Human creativity is still essential in decision-making, particularly in areas that require innovation and problem-solving. Effective collaboration between humans and machines can ensure that both data-driven insights and human creativity are taken into account, leading to better outcomes and greater innovation.

4. **Human-machine collaboration can lead to better outcomes:** Studies have shown that effective collaboration between humans and machines can lead to better outcomes than either humans or machines could achieve alone. By leveraging the strengths of both, organizations can make better decisions and achieve better results.

Human-machine collaboration is a growing trend in today's fast-paced and technology-driven world. With the advancement of technology, machines are becoming increasingly capable of performing complex tasks that were once the sole domain of humans. At the same time, humans bring their unique abilities, such as creativity, intuition, and empathy, to the table.

Studies have shown that when humans and machines work together in collaboration, they can achieve better outcomes than either could achieve alone. This is because humans and machines have different strengths and weaknesses, and when combined, they can complement each other and compensate for each other's limitations.

For example, human workers may have excellent problem-solving skills and experience, but they may not be able to process vast amounts of data as quickly or accurately as a machine. On the other hand, a machine may be able to process data quickly and accurately, but it lacks the contextual understanding, emotional intelligence, and creativity of a human.

By leveraging the strengths of both humans and machines, organizations can make better decisions and achieve better results. For example, in the healthcare industry, the use of ML algorithms to analyze patient data has led to improved accuracy in diagnosis and treatment recommendations. In manufacturing, the use of collaborative robots (cobots) has increased productivity and efficiency while reducing human error.

However, effective collaboration between humans and machines requires careful consideration of several factors. One crucial factor is trust. Humans must trust that machines will perform their tasks correctly, and machines must be programmed to recognize and respond to human input appropriately.

Another important factor is communication. Humans and machines must be able to communicate effectively with each other to ensure that they are working towards the same goals. This can be achieved through the use of natural language processing and other communication technologies.

Collaboration between humans and machines has the potential to produce better results than either species could produce on its own. Organizations can make better decisions, increase efficiency, and produce better outcomes by combining the advantages of both. However, in order for collaboration to be successful, trust, communication, and other factors must be carefully taken into account. To make this collaboration possible, organizations must spend money on the necessary technology and training.

In a world where machines are increasingly making decisions, efficient human-machine collaboration is essential. Humans and machines can make better decisions, ensure that ethical considerations are taken into account, and produce better results than either could do on their own when they work together effectively.

Freeson U. Eze is a multifaceted individual with a deep understanding of the high-tech industry. As a seasoned web designer and app developer, he has made significant contributions to the digital landscape. His expertise extends beyond technology; he is also a business personality with a keen insight into the evolving dynamics of the corporate world. In addition to his professional achievements, Freeson is a dedicated pastor and preacher, committed to spreading spiritual teachings and positively impacting the lives of many. His unique blend of technical knowledge, business acumen, and spiritual leadership makes him a distinguished voice in discussing the intersection of machine learning and executive leadership.

www.ingramcontent.com/pod-product-compliance
Lightning Source LLC
Chambersburg PA
CBHW061333120726
48001CB00002B/829